Rain Drops

The Poetry of Jack Darby Rider

Rain Drops

The Poetry of Jack Darby Rider

Sidekick Press
Bellingham, Washington

Published 2021
Printed in the United States of America
ISBN 978-1-7344945-8-7
LCCN 2020925457

Sidekick Press
2950 Newmarket Street
Suite 101-329
Bellingham, WA 98226
https://sidekickpress.com

Rain Drops: The Poetry of Jack Darby Rider

Cover Design: Spoken Designs – spokendesigns.com

DEDICATION

To my mother . . .
Born Ione Grace Darby, Mom raised two children
with little help from my father. Loving, supporting,
and forgiving—her standard for a good life, she never
fell short on her responsibilities.

See "Feelings" page 78.

CONTENTS

RAIN DROPS

*A mirror tells tales, on the reflections of your life or those
around you, depending on which side you are on.*

Seattle

Overcast with shards of rain,
    a fog descending on my brain,
        when will it ever shine again? I prattle.
Although the weather's not so hot,
    complaining will improve it not,
        acclimatizing helps, so goes the battle.

I'm puddle-bred and puddle-born,
    my feet are webbed, galoshes worn;
        with all this chaser, who could e'er get tight?
My hands are wrinkled all the time,
    I dried out once in '69,
        that dry spell lasted almost overnight.

So if you'd like to visit here,
    and do it when the weather's clear,
        on August fourth it sometimes warms a little.
But if you're not the chancy type,
    don't come out here to chew and gripe,
        just leave me soaking sunshine in Seattle.

Nature's Way

The sky outside was clear today
    while rain was coming down;
a paradox of nature's way
    it fell upon the town.
How can it rain when reason says
    this simply can't be so?
From clearly cloudless azure hue,
    Precipitation? No!
Yet down it came—this nonexistent
    wetness chilling through.
And I got wet and cold
    and I turned nonexistent blue!

The Drizzle on My Doorstep

Often when the sky turns gray
    and drizzle dogs the door,
my attitude will follow
    in a way most folks abhor;
a snarling pitter-pat
    of petty troubles by the score,
that's the time I need remember
    what my Higher Power's for.

Not to supplement my pocket
    tho my bankbook's kinda grim;
not to titillate my sex life,
    it seems that's much too trim,
but to turn it to a shower
    like when spring's a seasonin';
from the drizzle on my doorstep
    comes abundance from within.

Rain

Rain, rain, soggy rain;
pummeling the roof,
saturating moss fresh green
among red asphalt shingles,
soggy, green, patchy intruders.

Droplets turn to rivulets
racing down the mottled patterns
stretching clear and elastic in liquid icicles,
saturating the earth below,
tracing a line beneath the eaves.

Reaching up, the earth accepts
this watery intrusion
without complaint
providing varied taxi services
through waterlogged soil
to creek, lake, river
and sea.

Through it all
the earth accepts
without a whimper
'though it sometimes rumbles
with the sounds of flooding;
and the movement of earth
too saturated to remain in place
any longer.

While we complain
about the inconvenience,
and the damage, the sunless skies;
the earth accepts the flow
without pause or quarrel.

The beauty of rain can best be seen
in the acceptance of its inconveniences . . .
As perhaps with other things in life.

Windstorm

Fir branches,
broken from the wind,
piled in disrespect,
beneath the trees;
birch leaves,
strewn helter-skelter;
sheets of newspaper
plastered against the fence,
corners pointing upwards in surrender;
the tops of both birches
dangle broken near the top
waiting for a day of industry,
for the ladder and the chain saw
and me.

Something inside says
I should not like the wind,
or the rain and the darkness;
the dankness of it all;
there's plenty to hide from;
the wind and the rain,
and the industry.

In the midst of it all,
snuggled in my blankets
listening to the wind against
the side of the house,
rain drumming on the roof,
running from the edge
in a cacophonous waterfall.
There's certainly enough
to not like.

But when are blankets more comforting?
When are sounds more acute?
And when am I more aware
of the warm presence beside me
bearing witness to a mutual need?

I think it helps to look again,
to seek the other side.
Looking broadly gives perspective to life
and imparts an appreciation
even of windstorms.

Gray

Overcast and dreary
clouds with gray edges
discernable as puffballs of moisture
pierced by mountaintops.

Swirling,
encompassing trees
breaking shape only slightly
at the edges.

Such images are
both dull and profound.

Cold and wet,
chilling and depressed
through fabric still clinging
to a warmer season
just passed.

Yet there's loveliness
in black and white;
not all things need color
to touch that sense of proportion
we perceive as beauty.

The inner senses look beyond
the gray edges
to an untapped spectrum
when viewed with an attitude
of surrender.

Autumn's Backyard

Yellow birch leaves,
green fir branches
fallen from the storm,
piled up for disposal;
curved concrete patio
lined with holly and azaleas,
old fiberglass roof
needing newness against the rain;
flowering plants:
impatiens and begonia,
beautiful last summer,
now limp in soggy autumn death;
grass, compacted with leaves,
needing one more mowing;
holes where Maggie dug,
deep enough to irritate,
not enough to anger.

Not much happens here
after the last raking.
It's left to the squirrels, and the birds
and Maggie,
who will reign
until the crocus
and the green-tipped branches
draw us out again
to the splendor of new growth—
the beginnings of another fall.

Bent Cottonwood

Bark deeply wrinkled,
an elephant's foreleg
rising to bend ten feet up,

pointing askew to Westward
following a sun's rays
in early morning.

Angled thirty degrees or more,
a divide points downward
bare and dead now;

The other stretching upwards
in perfect health.
refusing to die.

Old growth grappling in twisted spasm
how long ago? Entertaining new life
stronger than the parent.

We are like that
surviving through our children.
They will bend.

It's painful to watch them.
Bend.
They will survive as we have.

Always reaching.
Always upwards.
Through their children.

Blue Sky

Is blue sky
a reflection of ourselves
or of others

whose experience must be
arranged differently
like scattered tumbleweeds

racing across open fields
or fallen apples
left rotting in limpid grass.

Such questions.
I don't know.
So much I don't know.

Why try to answer
what is truly unseen.
Does the unseen

become seen
when I express it?
I wonder?

OF THE SPIRIT

*Vision belongs to those who learn to see
without using their eyes.*

On Religion

Could God but make me understand
    this feeling deep in me;
Could he but fathom, breach for me
    what my soul tries to see.
Could I but see through eyes of those
    who say they understand;
Could I but worship with the rest,
    could I extend my hand
In loving faith, with soul laid bare,
    my thoughts and eyes most humble,
my heart within assuring me
    that I could never stumble.
Could I? Could they? I wish. I pray.
    Patience, will you reward me?

But then, could they but see as I?
    I wonder. What would they see?

A Consensus

Dawn amends what did offend
    when twilight passed away,
Each fading glow tucked far below
    horizon's distant bend.
As darkness darkens, thoughts contrive
    to light what must sustain
our homoeostatic consciousness
    'til dark is forced to wane.
What keeps this inner balance
    while immortal's light transcends?
We think we know the answer
    and, my guess is, guesses blend.

Reckoning Path

The nearing comes for reckoning
    as daily on is seen,
our path upon life's timely trail
    is set from infancy.
We wonder where its course began
    and why it travels near,
as if its brief meanderings
    were meant for us to hear.

The positive look forward
    beyond a distant bend;
the hesitant stand sideways
    to cover either end;
and some look only backwards
    down the path from whence they came,
as if to cover up those steps
    that trod on tender stem.

But how we choose to travel
    or how true each course may be,
as sure as its beginnings
    to the end we'll never see;
and should our presence matter
    with each passing step, 'til then;
these answers here we'll never view:
    to where, from whence, nor when.

Moss

Moss is independent
or at least irregular.
It grows on the north sides
of trees and things
living in twilight.

Some regard it as decay
living on dead things.
All other matter abides
in the fetal warmth of the sun
and the intra-reliance
of one being upon another.

But moss.
Moss shares an inter-dependence
with earthly things
beyond Polaris' spectral way.

A Twinkling

Life's a simple moment in a time that goes beyond
    the most extreme horizon my mind can ponder on.
Yet, I cling so desperately to intransigent things,
    and miss a million others from which daily living springs.

Life is but a moment and still I squander time,
    in meaningless meanderings my mind obsesses on.
From dillydally wanderings to salve a mindless trail,
    possessed upon a tempest thought, experience prevails.

So when my cherished moment comes I'll pray a guileless prayer;
    the simple taste of love on table set with kindness fared.
With peace in all relationships; with faith, and hope, and care.
    My legacy upon this Earth, a daily trust to share.

Ivy

Ivy moving endlessly
   on vacant house and wall.
Ivy crawling constantly,
   brief holdings neat and small.
Always climbing, seeking,
   finding nothing but the fall.
Ivy, trying timelessly.
   I ponder. Is that all?

Hassayampa

Mysterious, underground,
flowing through sand and rock
cutting stone canyons
impervious to green.

Broad, swirling sandy river
devoid of water
surrounded by cholla, ocotillo,
Joshua tree, stately saguaro
and brown.

So different from
tall, stately northwest trees
familiar to me and mine.

Dry riverbed
coursing invisibly
through a desert landscape
leaving broad, entwined ripples
through sun-hardened land.

Lovely in its
accumulated differences;
stunning by day
or in moonlight;
enduring in its humanity.

THOUGHTS

*Patience allows you
to possess your goals
before they are attained, if ever.*

On Giving Advice

If you can tell me where to go
    without a smart reply,
and know that's where I oughta be,
    well, maybe, I might try.
But choose directions carefully—
    make sure it's not a quirk.
'Cause what if you are wrong my friend?
    Or worse, it just might work!

Full Circle

There must be a simple prayer
    for times when thought is bent
on rendering an epitaph
    upon some hapless gent
whose only crime committed,
    least as far as I can see,
was in doing it the same darn way
    as I do when it's me!

Working it Through

I resent intrusion
    from the guy who's calling leads,
from glorious self-appointment,
    to intrude upon my deeds;
whose seeming intuition probes,
    though seldom sanely sought,
and, though most well-intentioned,
    raises havoc with my thoughts.

There's one thing I can count on,
    my resentment clearly seen;
decisively defensive,
    stoic now, like in a dream;
if he would only stop to think
    instead of heading true,
I'd help him see it my way.
    MY WAY! Well, I worked that through.

Gratitude

Gratitude means listening
    to a fear so long suppressed,
I'm often sorely tempted
    to resist the kind caress
tendered me by someone
    dear enough to understand,
yet still remain attentive—
    closer still we seem to band.

One voice says his listening
    is the key to my success.
But then awareness turns and I find
    I am saying less.
This processed intuition
    gratitude alone can see;
the insight I'm most grateful for:
    I'm listening to me!

Midlife Crisis

Life's contented hour
is lost without repose
and fearing years' unkind investiture
runs unhappily
from one imposter
to another.

The only sanity,
an awareness
that thinking too much
is a mindless pastime.

Time

The sum of existence
belabored by thought and examination;
recurring trial of judgment, value,
and moral cause;
intellectualizing
'til exhaustion brings simplicity.

The knowledge that
whatever was or will be
is not of our will.

The fortunate find acceptance.
The grand search ends and begins.
A timelessness culminating
. . . in today.

Mindlessness

Windowless, airless, stuffy,
engaging the hot fog of summer
in the wintertime;
no one to turn to but myself.

Where is the relief?
Why must I constantly fidget
within my imagination?
Is it an inborn insanity;
am I just naturally boppo?

My head spews nonsense;
the stuff that adds confusion to dreams.
Is it really without sense
or a kind of unsense?
Perhaps the reasoning of some things
just seems insane.

Sometimes, to view my mind
from its inner side
is a frightening experience.
Is this what schizophrenia is all about?
No, that's when you live there
in the reality of the unreal.
And my reality is that it bugs me.

My thoughts scan a faraway horizon
and become impaled upon my fears.
Is this truly unreal
or just the meandering
of an old fool?

No. I'm not old enough.
Yet!

The Presence of a Friend

There's just no substitution for the presence of a friend
    tho wives and others try to find their way.
When solitude is lonely and your worries have no end,
    a buddy has the care that can transcend.

If unrest stands beside you and your partner can't amend
    the ache within persisting through the day;
When every pat solution's out of reach beyond the bend,
    there's just no substitution for a friend.

The Right

In wonder of the symbol dove,
    peacemakers plan the Right.
Police dispel the students quell,
    onlookers view the Right.
Thousands die in Idol's eye
    as leaders claim the Right.
If man is there without despair,
    is Right incarnate plight?

Homemade Wine

I hadn't found a name for it
    I couldn't call it "Cherry,"
Although the maraschino jar
    was added, thanks to Terri.
'Cause mostly it's got peach juice,
    oh, and apricot and pearie,
And since this rhyme's ridiculous
    I'll call it "Farkelberry."

OF THE EARTH

Solitude is great listening,
until you get an earful.

Taneum Creek

Taneum Creek in autumn
    where cottonwoods abound,
and elderberry bushes glow
    with purple bunches round;
Where yellow rustles gently
    to the frost-forgotten ground,
Taneum Creek in autumn
    brings the richest blessings down.

Goose Prairie

Before Mazama ceased to be,
the prairie was there.

Led by brief holdings of lichen and moss
hiding timidly in the quiet places,
vanguard for fern and other low growth.
Meager multitudes mingled for survival long before
fir, pine, hemlock, tamarack, and spruce arrived
giving the impression that majesty led the way.

In timely fashion,
an opening appeared in kingly canopy;
below the lake, but not a lake,
for a slope is there,
and a steady seepage flows underneath,
fed from the ridge rising to the north
over two thousand feet from prairie floor.

Royal conquerors began a gradual retreat
from this insidious invasion
of prairie grass and yarrow,
though it had stood to the edge
before there was an edge.
The prairie must have been too grand
even before.

A timid onslaught
led by the quiet and unseen,
camp followers of the grand glacial retreat.

The meek loan on long-term leases
with insidious escape clauses
to benefit the timid.

Kings are kings because they appear to be
and are eventually dispossessed.
They'd do well to learn the art of surrender
from prairies.

Skagit Bay

Heavy grass,
roots buried deep in soft mud
along the edge of the bay;
small holes reveal
soft shell, butter and horse clams;
life teeming in muck
that captures the feet,
sucking them down
into the brown abyss.
Rubber boots draw heavily,
pulling slowly, ever so slowly,
each step an effort
straining muscle,
pulling boot over heel,
piling socks around toes.

The tide flows,
filling, swirling,
covering feet seeking firmness,
hurrying as the shoreline races
towards the heavy grass.

Snow geese, mallard, wigeon, teal,
overhead, on the skyline,
coming and going,
this way and that
in organized disarray,
anticipating the safety of the bay.

December's light on the horizon,
afternoon late at four o'clock,
white light under gray, moist clouds,
streaks of light blue and pink,
seasonal twilight
giving a hint of warmer times.

Back at the car,
boots and bulky clothing put away,
the view now from the shore,
pink light vague in the distance—
as evening comes to Skagit Bay
until another time.

The Annual Hunting Trip

The last week in October
the leaves near Winthrop
are yellow and gold,
tinged with brown.
Only a hint of green remains
in memory of the season just passed.

I walk the hills in green wool pants
that blend with the trees
and a bright orange hat and vest
that doesn't.

I love to walk the hills
dreaming of ages past.
Several thousand years ago
before Mazama blew
an ancient Indian
looked down the Methow
or the Chewack
at the same telling hues of
yellow, brown, and leftover green.
Perhaps he sat on the rock
where I now sit.
But not for long.
The rock holds cold
from the previous night.
I feel it through my green wool pants.

My ancient friend
would choose a log
or a tuft of bunch grass.
He didn't have my pants
to stem the chill.

It helps to join
the previous centuries
with the present.
It's so much to peruse:
this insidious timelessness.

The deer must be grateful;
it's not often I fill my tag.

Fort Ebey in Winter

Pastoral,
quiet, peaceful,
green grass in winter
Surrounded by tall evergreens:
hemlock and Douglas fir.
A flicker flies from the ground
sitting partly up a tree
to survey—mostly me.
There's no one else;
the quiet is unbroken.

My eyes turn upwards above the trees
two hundred feet tall
to a light blue sky.
There, above all, an eagle soars
in slowly moving circles.
I watch for several minutes
a serenely revolving corkscrew
moving infinitely towards me.

He's so high.
How can he see the detail I know he can see.
I watch him through several rotations.
His wings never move—only his head.
I see him looking—even as high as he is.
Not a sound. No screech.
No whistling of the wings.
He's too high.

I wonder
Is this God watching over everything?
Truly beautiful.
White head and tail.
Watching.
Looking.
Waiting to kill something.

A Sonnet on the Bumping

First light prances over Nelson's Ridge.
Pines, whose ruddy reddish bark stirs hope
in subtle silence on opposite slope,
respond in waking to Lucia's airy bridge.
Amber reflects to near stands lair,
where firs in prominence wait their turn
since coned seeds fell to shaded burn
so long ago, as timeless lots forbear.

Now cottonwood and willow green
shudder in waiting as the Bumping flows
in gentle cadence, respecting the serene.
Those lastly standing show their mien
    against all who would allot them blows,
    and, with patience, then offset the scene.

Sailing Pond

Glisten has the sound for it
    with surface sparkling new;
and then the boats they're sailing,
    several sails of white and blue.
The breeze that adds the riffle
    has its own importance too.
As does the sun, let's not forget;
    just that, and me and you.

Lodgepole vs. Tamarack

Lodgepole Pine
tall, straight,
needles little round puffballs
on short branches
bark crusted over
like too dry bread
or skin on the very old.

An occasional Tamarack
just as straight
but taller
needles like spider webs on branches
arching slightly upwards.

The former holds needles year-round
while the latter sheds all in fall
covering the ground in
a rust-covered blanket

So similar
yet so different.
Each and all
living together
peacefully
until a strong wind
or winter snow
throws one awkwardly against the other
breaking the peace of those around.

People live like that.
In peace.
Until one is uprooted
and challenges the boundaries
of another.

When a tree falls
injury occurs
and disruption ends.
There's no retribution.
No revenge.
They just let nature do its thing.

Why can't people do that?
Could there be something to this
"Turn the other cheek" business.

But no.
People are much too smart
and well-educated
and spiritually superior
for that.

Skagit Fields

Daffodils beginning to sparkle,
yellow showing sparsely
among fields of dark green.
Air crisply fresh, chilly
    from previous night's raindrops.

Driving up quiet
past ice cream stand
just opened on Fir Island;
    busy with spring searchers.

Snow geese busily stocking up,
broad white blanket,
drifting from one flock to another,
    never-ending disarray.

Rexville store, still, but open,
waiting for tourists descending
to tulips in a few weeks
    or less.

But now daffodils.
    First true hint.

Shortly, whole valley
exploding with yellow
to harken a multitude of color,
heralding imminent domain
    of Tulip Fields.

    It really is spring.

The Fisherman

I tried to catch a fish today
    I have a certain style
It's one I've long developed
    O'er many a knotty mile.
I've purchased all the proper gear
    With pole and line so neat
And then this boat and motor
    She's the envy of the fleet.
I've hooked up with anchovies
    Also hoochies and a spoon
And then a plug, one that's designed
    To make a salmon swoon.
How could I lose, you'd wonder
    With all the stuff I've bought
I went to bed the night before
    Enmeshed in total thought.
I reviewed preparations
    But found it hard to sleep
And when I finally woke I found
    I'd also missed the fleet.
They went ahead without me
    And returned with all those fish
They held forth at the cleaning rack
    While I could only wish.
Now I may have solved the problem
    The solution I can see
I'll focus on the evening bite
    The one that's made for me.

Arachnid

Cocoon-like nests burst into morning,
warm sun nourishment,
firming legs no longer bound.

A brief resting, awareness,
propelled by an inner silent voice,
life's perennial activity begins.

Moving up a near, tallest tree,
then, reaching out on a limb
to its apex.

Firm attachment, letting go,
falling, suspended by silver strands,
tiny in imperceptibility.

Now, together, pushed
by some insistent timepiece,
shimmering threads descend.

I was sleeping when one attached
to my side mirror, quietly,
without sound or perceived motion.

Such energy and innate dedication,
moving from one point to another,
working in utter silence.

Three points attached, then
inner workings, an outline as
form begins to emerge.

Like spokes of a wagon wheel,
concentric rings of shimmering net
to trap an unsuspecting victim.

When I arrive it's done, amazing.
I almost don't open the door,
but I do.

He'll start again. Hopefully
in a safer place. Or not.
But he'll start again.

Bumping in June

Walking towards lake
from campground visited often

before. Surface shimmers
between trees. Reservoir full

now. Logs and stumps
piled along shore. Many since first

cut in 1911. Later, lake recedes
behind dam with waterlogged

wood drying in warm August
sun, brittle tinder to any spark.

But now June, seasonal warmth,
forest green and damp. Returning,

I see four kids playing. My kids.
Chip dancing among them. Jill,

youngest, straight blonde hair,
keeping up. David, fire builder,

gathering wood, Linda, Mark, busy,
creating some new adventure. Chip, gone

now thirty years. Mark, accomplished
sailor, Linda, beautiful music, writer,

David, energetic, striving. All still
loving the outdoors, but too busy.

Grown, adult, respectful. Yet I see only
children, and Jill, gone, breast cancer.

All my children; love rising
within me hard to contain.

Tears flow, aging tears
of memory. Thanks

for memory.

Summer Sunrise in Yakima

Morning comes clearly.
Stars dim and disappear
seeking shelter in darkened space.

Overhead darkness
despairs to grayness.
Dim reflections clear the way.

Softness comes in hints of blue.
A robin's egg reflection
in morning's clear beginnings.

Warm light on the horizon.
A rising of a shade anticipating
sudden life giving brightness.

Sky now full blue,
Long shadows stripping away
morning's dew.

With it a crisp clearness,
Cool yet.
Heat of day will come soon enough.

But now, that clearness of sight.
Signaling what? New day? Good day?
Peaceful, warm, delicious day.

The Hummingbird

Poised in flight, hesitant
before the feeder rail.
Watchful, looking for others,
long stiletto beak, waiting.

Then plunging to the sweetness
of man-made nectar.
Others come for sustenance
and are repulsed.

Rushing to fill their needs,
four and five together.
A pulsing gaggle
of mighty hummers.

Battle lines drawn
as evening comes
and darkness prevails.
Defending beyond his fill.

He'll be back tomorrow.
I must refill the nectar
before tomorrow's battle.
Diurnal pleasures.

LOVE AND FAMILY

Love comes
When you have the patience to see it
And the tolerance to accept it.

Early Love

As winter falls to memory
    and springtime's flower grows true,
my thoughts return to early love
    and how it also grew.
And when, as summer's fullest bloom
    foretells of autumn's gold,
those memories of early love
    within my heart unfold.

For early love is wondrous;
    it taps the inner throng,
and fills the soul harmoniously
    with youngest manhood's song.
But, as the seasons go their way,
    this knowledge, too, will sing;
early love's fulfillment comes
    with later manhood's spring.

Renewal

Patio planters,
old, rotted through,
left by a spinster aunt,
long gone.

"They should be thrown away."

She agreed with acquiesced eyes.

Hosed and dried,
old and mold brushed off,
wood seen and
new bottoms stapled on,
still needing more.

The paint shelf failed to suppress
a can of red latex enamel,
risky bright for heirlooms.
Red on the brush.
Red on old wood,
and me.

Planter quickly dried and replaced,
I led her out
to see if she'd be pleased,
worried the brightness
would be too much
even for acquiescence.

I don't know
if she took
to the color.
But she took very much
to me.

Table Flowers

They came quietly,
a bright flourish
hindering passage
past the check stand.

No reason.
I could have passed easily
but for the pervasiveness
of her liking for them.

Home, a brightened table
filled with affinity.

Days passed and color dried as
loving hesitation slowed the removal
of memoried senses.
They lasted almost two weeks.
Too long for cut things?

Such holdings on
sustain affection
far beyond the freshened tenure
of table flowers.

What's New?

What else is new?
New?
My love for you?
No, that's been going on for quite some time now.
In fact, I think I've always loved you.
Always.

I guess it just seems so.
The newness of some things just won't wear.

Every year.
Every hour.
Every precious moment.
I love you.

The Sanding of Time

Precious little escapes the sanding of time.

We met and courted;
that was fun
most of the time.
Coffee dates,
the trip to Whidbey Island;
a wedding,
and a honeymoon in the mountains.
Such neat memories.
Then college, kids, career,
there've been so many careers.

And then the painful times.
The long, hurtful times.
And the waiting.

It would seem there shouldn't be painful times.
But if there weren't
we might not appreciate
the time we have now.
And the time I have with you is appreciable.

The sanding of time
adds a luster
that makes the courting part
so much better.

Waiting for Solitude

I wait for solitude,
through the hurt
and the frustration
and the not knowing.
It's hard to get through it,
this feeling of unsettledness
that forms on my diaphragm,
sitting there,
no place to go.

Why can't it pass?
Like the wind on a warm summer's evening,
or evanescent thoughts quickly forgotten.

You, lest I forget to say
are the balm,
the antithesis to all anxiety;
You, warm and caring,
withholding comment.
Especially without comment.

My love.

The Collingwood Table

The estate sale
beckoned from the farmhouse
shaded behind locust trees
near Waitsburg.
Cars waited in the stubble,
eight or ten neatly parked.

Things were scattered in ragged order;
farm things, homey things
displayed about the yard and drive.
We looked, but not long,
before our eyes focused
on the dismembered pieces
of a round oak table.
Dirty and scarred, marred with
splotches of paint from some lost project,
a drill hole in the center from another.
Behind, a rough-hewn box with broken slats
contained six leaves.
But the price tag said three-fifty.

So we drove on to Dayton,
enjoying the scenes of harvest
and our time together.

Coming back, the table wouldn't let us pass.
Should we make a bid?
Terri always wanted one
like grandmother Walker's,
and I, too, like grandad Darby's.
The farmer's wife told us
the table had been purchased
by her Grandfather Collingwood in 1917
for his 1893 farm.

70

Her father and mother were there:
inheritors of the Collingwood table;
theirs since 1925;
theirs for over sixty years;
theirs, you could tell.
He talked family history to me
while she stood in her walker
next to my pickup,
her hand on the dark stained wood;
touching it,
stroking it gently.

On impulse we paid full price.
Or was it a toll?
Most certainly
it was an act of love.

Silence of the Heart

When the ache falls deep within my being,
My insides simply can't endure;
When light recedes from every bright reminder,
And gentle strains go listlessly away;
When all those things that made a subtle difference,
Seem distant and apart from all I know;
And I am lost without a place to turn to,
I turn to see who's waiting, just to see.

You're there, although you may not be so knowing,
Just your presence brings a sense of calm;
The stain of sorrow can't seep through your aura,
The pain of things just simply won't intrude.
You may never know my sense of being,
Or feel the sadness I alone must feel,
But you have made it all the more revealing,
To know all love through silence of the heart.

In Retrospect

I equate with ferrous things
    my elder's thoughts on life;
For I am wont to criticize
    what wasn't learned through strife.
But certain things I do perceive
    to offer my respect:
My father's hand, my mother's eye,
    and Grandpap's poker deck.

My grandfather was the most important man in my life. He wasn't a large man, about 5'6" I suppose, and completely bald since his twenties. He grew up in the wilds of Eastern Oregon and provided me with many tales of his upbringing including an 1896 bank robbery in Joseph, Oregon, he personally witnessed. Some stories I hesitate to repeat.

Once, when I was twelve, he enlisted me to help him with a carpentry job he had contracted for another family member. When the day was done, we were to spend the night in the building (I don't know why). He paid me a silver dollar for my day's "work."

As we chatted, he asked if I would like to play some cards. I couldn't see why not so I agreed. That's when I learned to play stud poker. Now you must understand I loved my grandfather very much. But at ten cents a hand, it didn't take long for him to relieve me of my silver dollar.

I remember being confused. I wasn't accustomed to this kind of game and that dollar sure disappeared in a hurry. I think that's when I learned the meaning of ambivalence. But I accepted his "lesson."

It's important to note that I've never been a gambler. Also, I've never had a problem accepting my own baldness, and I've been bald since my thirties. He was truly one of a kind.

Love Will Turn and Go

A tree stood in a meadow
    with blossoms in the spring,
I saw my love with shining eyes,
    her hand touched mine, our breath drew sighs.
Then spring drew nigh to summer,
    the tree grew green and strong.
As love unfolds our hearts grew bold
    and pressed our love within its fold.

Trees will blossom and love will grow,
    then, as the leaves, love will turn and go.

Now fall with all its splendor,
    fruit ripens in the sun.
Our love was strong, intense too long,
    as fruit o'er-ripened wanes its song.
For winter's 'round the corner,
    the leaves are on the ground.
My love so fair with flowing hair
    has fallen with my heart's despair.

Trees will blossom and love will grow,
    then, as the leaves, love will turn and go.

The tree stands on the meadow,
  white frost upon its hair.
A chill prevails our lovers' trails,
  our thoughts, my dreams, to windward sail.
Will springtime bring another;
  will warmth I feel again?
Will I, but then when winter's done
  the tree will blossom with the sun.

Trees will blossom and love will grow,
  then, as the leaves, love will turn and go.

Genesis

Her mother's hair,
my mother's eyes,
my son's impish grace.
Twin ponytails to match
corners of a mouth
made for happiness.

His two teeth bite through purée
of fruit and cereal
spread from nose to chin
and dimple to dimple.
He looks like me, they say.
I don't argue.

Accurately bright,
she names body parts
from an adult text
for her aunt in med school,
but can't sit still,
proclaiming answers
without hesitation
in voice or limb.

Could this creation
be more lovely than
my firstborn and
his successors?

Only this.
My grandchildren.
He's four months;
she just turned eight.

Comparison beyond measure.
Bested perhaps in generations
not envisioned by today's
most consummate standards.

Without prejudice
of course.

Feelings

Listen to your feelings
    though your mind hears something else;
Listen, as your heart and soul
    in simple silence swell.
Listening is an art perceiving;
    thinking merely knows.
But feelings, neither right nor wrong,
    bring perspicacious glows.

My mother was many things. She raised my sister and me with little help from my father but was always there for us. Her relationship with her parents and her high school education resulted in a person with exceptional ability, well beyond what one might expect. But the one attribute I most respected was her ability with words. She was literally a walking dictionary.

This was a ready resource for me. I wasn't very good with words or spelling. English wasn't my favorite subject growing up. Whenever I ran into a difficult word, I would simply ask Mom. No matter what I came up with, she could spell it and tell me what it meant.

Eventually, this became a challenge. But she never failed. Finally, one day, I heard a word that I just knew would get her. It was a glorious word; one that was destined to bring this competition to a shining crescendo.

"Perspicacity." It means "of keen and discerning mind."

I couldn't wait to get home. As I presented it to her, she simply smiled, spelled it, and told me what it meant. It was just too much. I started to giggle and then laugh. She responded in kind, and we descended into hysterics.

For years afterward, whenever I saw that word in print, I would cut it out and send it to her without any indication of who had sent it. Once, it even appeared in the comic strip "Tumbleweeds."

I wrote this poem for her.

Toolboxes

Corners, cubicles,
resting places for wrenches,
punches, screwdrivers, sockets,
pliers with curved, long noses,
and portability.

Found among tackle boxes,
mine helped me learn
when a costlier mechanic
was out of the question.
It fixed the furnace
that time below zero,
and it manufactured toys at Christmastime
without directions.

There's less cause for mending now.
Kids grow into their own toolboxes.
Time eventually broke a bracket;
defied fixing in the fixer.

Then this spring there it was;
clean, new, a bit larger,
but portable for ready action.

Tools cleaned, sorted,
better placed, ample space,
looked at, admired, admired again,
in manifest repair.

There's a twinge as I set the old box aside,
insides worn, dirty, empty,
broken bracket dangling loosely
beyond a mend.
I found some odd thing to store in it—
placed it away to avoid letting go.

I think it must be all right.
My most used things
are stored.

Bridal Dresses

Bridal dresses
low necklines and no necklines
lace and pearls and silk
and less
none in true simplicity
but all white
in deference to the obvious

My daughter
my youngest offspring
the achiever
very considerate
most of the time
very lovely
and not just to me
athletic
tenacious to a fault
deeply in love with a young man
I didn't pick
thank God

They've lived together for a year
that's how it's done now
I think it's only a minor change

It was scary to look at bridal gowns
on a mannequin
or in a magazine

So we looked at our album
thirty-eight years old
It helped to remember
and brought a flood of warmth
so intense it erased all fears

I've really done well you know!

The Light Won't Go Out

The light won't go out.
It was there that January.
Tiny, soft, imperceptibly lovely.
Sparkling even then.
Transmitting loveliness.

Trailing her brothers and sister.
Always keeping up.
But softly.
And quietly.
A sparkle through a lighted room.

In school, quietly independent.
Searching, working, always making friends.
The "Barbie years" with Janet, Anna, and Beth.
A peacemaker, sharing, a constant love.
Commanding General of the school safety patrol.
Soft, earnest leadership.

An inspiration in cross-country.
A charger coxswain on Husky Crew.
Always thinking of ways to instill.
Then the preparation for med school.
Earnest, unsure, but determined.
Never first in line, but there at graduation.

Working hard to earn her residency.
Meeting Tim.
Coming for Christmas.
Hiding the seriousness of their relationship.
The marriage and that hated phrase,
"I get to die first."

Breast cancer, surgery, chemo,
The time at home.
Fearful but determined.
Then remission.
And Annelise.
Delightful Annelise.

Then reoccurrence.
Letting go of the practice.
Concentrate on Anna, family,
And a deep searching awareness
Of things beyond her grasp.
Finding a peace and sharing it.

Guiding her family to the very last.
All of us together.
Holding her.
The breathing stopped but the heart kept going.
For awhile.
Then no more.

But the light won't go out.
Love, Dad.

Child's Song

A child sings,
sees birds and wings
and clings.

Youngsters range
through endless change
while patience wanes.

Elders prize
to criticize
with sighs.

Why yearn for prime?
Assess the time
in rhyme.

The years unwind
when gentle mind
is kind.

Tears of Joy or Sorrow

Who has not shared the tears of joy
or of sorrow. And to whom do we look
when things are great, like a grandchild
smiling when he looks into your eyes,
or the pain that comes with sudden words
stabbing into your soul
like a knife slitting the belly of a fish;
the pangs of a well-meaning comment
merely too honest to accept
at the moment.

I think it's not an either-or.
Can't the two go together,
joy and sorrow?
Can we truly experience one
without the other?
Up without down;
in without out;
happy without sad.

Love and hate, the two play-actor masks
of a Greek tragedy. It seems counter,
to accept one with the other. Yet
in every case love embodies both
when I accept,
though I always must question
along the way.

In Reflection

The view came on so quickly;
    where did the minutes go?
The vision of that coffee date
    we had so long ago.
I still can see you stepping
    off the stairs and down the walk;
That's the first time when I saw your eyes;
    that's when I start the clock.

That first year in Seattle
    held many happy times;
but then there was uncertainty
    to test as union binds.
Somehow we held together
    and as the union grew,
we both decided passion
    wasn't all that made it true.

So on with the adventure,
    school, and then the children came;
With Mark and Linda, Dave and Jill,
    I don't know who's to blame.
Somehow or else we managed;
    on just one income, too.
You stayed at home to be there
    when the kids came home from school.

Five years in four apartments,
    thirty-nine in our first home;
and then we had a dog (dear Chip)
    who seemed to want to roam.
We watched 'em to adulthood;
    to college: science and math;
except for mighty Dave
    who had to choose a different path.

But looking back they've all done well,
    their talents stand them tall;
and now we've got three grandkids;
    near enough to fill this hall.
I only wish dear Jill were here;
    but life's not at an end;
Thank God we have each other;
    that and family and these friends.

Coffeehouses

Tully's, Fidalgo Bay, Starbucks,
Camano Island Roasters,
each hawking its own as
stifled carnival huckster or
corner newsboy in muted voice.

A magical fad, another
intrusion into daily life, or
an insertion of hidden quality,
spiritual overtones adding
dimension not yet clear.

If I sit here long enough, I might
justify almost any thought or surmise.
It's fun sitting here, mindless or
full of query, loading up on caffeine,
writing on my notebook computer.

Reading a book or newspaper.
It's warm, the pastry case is full
and tempting. Avoiding temptation,
the core of my station in life.
They do look good.

I resist.
I do. I do.
Another coffee, please.
I'll order looking up.
Away from the pastry case.

Skandia

There's a hubbub here at noontime,
hungry patrons come and go;
orders placed from hanging menus,
salads, sandwiches, and soups.
Food to die for, I'm not kidding,
there's a self-help coffee bar.
Those displays of pies and cookies,
quite unfit for faint-at-heart.
All us calorie-challenged chubbies
line up two deep at the bar.
It don't count to try the samples;
one or two can't really hurt.
'cause the reason why I come here?
Free Wi-Fi, well don't y'know!!!
Could there be another reason?
No! But could I try one more?

Winds at Bumping Lake

Trees bend and whisper
ever so softly;
breath, warm and loving,
moves past your ear,
building to awaken
warm, loving strength
touching that inner self.

In late afternoon,
winds off the Cascade Crest
drive down the valley
past sheer cataracts of
stone and firmament
belayed briefly by
virgin forest standing firm.

Thundering through all to reach
Bumping Lake's upper end,
moving to clear openness,
sweeping swiftly over
once blue-green surface
whipped into monstrous waves,
surprising boaters with its ferocity.

Assaulting trees at lake's lower end,
violent air is softened by lodge pole, tamarack,
standing firm against this perilous challenge.
I step from trees to face this airy onslaught,
strong but strangely soothing
against my face.

In winter, wind force strong,
returns in repeated challenge
drifting snow and blowing down
centuries old trees having withstood
frozen windblasts before.
Such is nature, stroking a placid scene
from more moderate times.

In summer, a gift against
a hot August afternoon.
Winter has beauty to be seen;
summer's beauty can be felt on cheeks,
a warm shiver down my backbone.
Such is the warmth of life.

The Iceman

Leather apron, ice tongs,
voice gruffy over cigar, well-chewed.
Odor heavy with every breath,

He speaks through clenched teeth,
smell wafting past my head
from his heavy, happy smile.

His pick chips flakes from a
Solid icy block for us kids
Waiting anxiously at his side.

Both hands hold tight for sucking.
Cheap ice cream in the warm sun.
I've always loved the smell of a well-chomped cigar.

Upper Bumping Falls

Up the Swamp Lake trail.
Not far, quarter-mile,
listen for soft sounds.

Cascading, glistening sound
through needled trees,
softening muted roar.

Turn from trail now,
downhill through tall trees
no trail to follow.

Steep, loose rocks
prevailing with each step
to be above, looking down.

Then final steep descent
below to emerging river.
Looking up, cascading stair steps.

River above turning
over rocky river falls,
white froth to pool below.

A columbine
shaded in green bushes
hiding in solitude.

A day's excursion
lovely in afternoon sun.
Reverent peace.

Tide

Tide flows unevenly
over the sand of memory.

Thoughts are blown hither-skither
in dimpled rows of discontent

on seeds of sorrow unbound.
above a blue coverlet of time

lies scattered by wind
streaming through all thought

meant to disavow
only me.

Fall Quarter

Sunny, September day
looking from an upstairs
coffee shop window,

milieu of caffeine sippers,
students, teachers, shoppers,
book readers and chatterers,

coffee drinks, cookies, muffins,
workbooks, studies, pencils,
notebooks, and notebook computers.

Fall quarter begins,
dress decidedly student, you can tell.
Levi's, tennis shoes, wrinkled shirts,

only the older men
button their sleeves,
tuck shirttails in.

the young, shirttails out,
tennies untied,
uniform of the day,

attitude of wonderment
and knowledge
amid a sea of ignorance.

I was there once.
Am I there still?
I wear loafers now.

The Trees at Ft. Ebey

Darkness prevails in Douglas fir
standing over two hundred feet

knurled by age and weather,
bark a weather vane of time gone,

holding firm through violent
off-the-strait's weather.

Seasonally bombarded by rain and wind,
bluff trees stand worn and bent,

malformed as Quasimodo against
this tumultuous onslaught.

Trunks reveal faces of terror
from the forest of Oz;

a haunted Halloween,
each daring to challenge the other,

deep, craggy likenesses,
scarred in timeless beauty.

Ready in a Minute

I'll be ready in a minute doesn't mean it.
Though she probably is thinking that it does.
She's gone back into the bathroom for a Kleenex
And her best intentions say that doesn't count.

You go open up the car and get it started.
That's a mantra that I've heard so many times.
If I do I'll just be sitting there impatient.
While she's gone and done some other mindless task.

I don't know why I think it could be different.
I've been down this path a thousand times before.
So I'll stand and wait and try to make her nervous
While she glares at me in stoic disconcert.

Now you may think I'm simply inconsiderate.
That my attitude and conduct aren't the best.
Well, maybe, but until I see it different.
Insanity does it over and over and over and over again.

The Fortune Cookie

The fortune cookie said,
"Express yourself, do something creative."
What can this man bring to the table?

I know I'm a man.
But what kind of a man?
A mean one?
A gentle one?
A cheap one?
A generous one?
An honest one?
One who struggles with the truth?
It's something to think about.

I like to be gentle;
but I can be mean.
I like to be generous;
but I can be cheap.
I respect honesty;
but sometimes my mouth
precedes my best intentions.

Funny how my mind works.
Creative?
Fortune cookies can be hazardous
to the ruminating mind.

Elliott Bay

I've never seen the Bay
    without a ferry in its midst,
And often more than one will trace
    a track where once was mist.
The shipyards and the port cranes
    at the southern edge are dressed
In orange hues to contrast
    with a blue-striped vessel's crest.
A grayness gives reminder that
    the navy's still around,
And, while waiting for completion,
    vacant decks give out no sound.
The downtown docks are busy
    with vacationers in shorts,
Who spend their dough on rattan chairs
    and paintings of the locks.
It's funny that the souvenirs
    collected at each stand,
Are mostly small-cast images
    hand-painted in Japan.
I guess this simple nonsense
    goes to show me all the more,
With Bainbridge in the distant west,
    and north, Magnolia's shore,
I'm not to take this seriously,
    especially not in May,
'Cause sunshine can do funny things
    To folks near Elliott Bay.

On Writing

Write
and the story will follow;
Perceive
and the characters will take form.
Tell the truth
and the character will emerge.

Tell it all:
the hurt,
the soiled,
and the downright dirty.

Love will also show through
as the darkness falls away
and resentment becomes boring
from being referred to too much.

Life remains
and exposes the soul to reality.
It ain't all bad!

The Voice

Where's the voice?
Is it here?
Or here?
Or down here?
What line is it?
Where does it change?
Is it sad?
Should it not be sad?

I don't know.
I don't know where it is
or where it's supposed to be.

But when I write about
my daughter
or my wife;
when I delve into
a reflection of my feelings,
into that area
I resist looking into,
I know where the voice is.
It's in me.

But too much of me is scary.
I can't expose too much.
Even if you like it
you might not like me.

So I control the voice.
Wouldn't you?

CPSIA information can be obtained
at www.ICGtesting.com
Printed in the USA
FSHW010615130321
79402FS